Ocean World

Contents

Why is Our Planet Blue?

Our planet looks blue when seen from outer space because nearly three-quarters of the Earth is covered by water. Our oceans support an enormous range of life, both above and below the surface – from hordes of seabirds to the fish of the deep.

In this book, you will read about creatures from all over our planet. Use the globes to find the part of the world where these animals live.

Some words in this book are shown in **bold**. These words are explained in the Glossary on pages 63 and 64.

Welcome to the Journey

The oceans affect every aspect of our lives. They influence our weather and provide an important source of food. The sea is both destroyer and provider; powerful enough to wreck ships with its waves, and gentle enough to provide a home for the tiniest sea creatures. Yet, despite the importance of the oceans, they remain mysterious. We have reached the Moon, but the deepest parts of our oceans have hardly been explored.

Beginning with the shore, this book will journey into deeper and deeper waters, eventually reaching 4,000 metres below the surface, where some remarkable discoveries have been made.

Life in the Sea

From the warm, shallow waters around the coasts to the frozen oceans at the poles, the sea teems with life. Plants and animals can survive even in the deepest parts of the ocean, where it is dark and bitterly cold.

The smallest life form in the sea, **plankton**, is an essential part of the diet of many sea creatures. Plankton is the name for plants and animals so tiny that they are swept to every part of the ocean by the **currents**. They provide a nutritious food source for other creatures. At the water's surface, **shoals** of fish eat the plankton. The fish, in turn, are eaten by bigger **predators**; these predators are then eaten by even bigger creatures, and so the process continues. This is called a **food chain**.

shoal of anchovetta

Plant plankton is vital to life on land as well as in the oceans – it produces 80 per cent of the oxygen in the air we breathe. The oxygen is released when the plant plankton makes its own food.

right: striped marlin and shoal of fish

A World of Facts

Did you know?

The average depth of the ocean is nearly four kilometres, but the average height of land is less than one kilometre above sea level. There is a vast underwater world that remains unexplored by humans.

There are mountain ranges underwater. The Mid-Atlantic Ridge is a chain of mountains in the middle of the Atlantic Ocean, extending more than 16,000 kilometres. That's nearly twice as long as the Andes Mountains in South America.

Record breakers

The largest ocean is the Pacific, which covers about one-third of the Earth's surface. Measuring nearly 180,000,000 square kilometres, the Pacific is larger than all the continents combined.

The Pacific is also the deepest ocean. Its average depth is 4,280 metres, but it reaches down as far as 11,033 metres.

The Blue whale is the largest animal ever to have lived, bigger even than the largest-known dinosaur. A Blue whale can weigh more than a group of 1,500 people. Its blood vessels are so big that a trout could swim through them, and its heart is as big as a small car.

Strange but true!

An undersea waterfall beneath the Denmark Straight sinks for over 3.5 kilometres – more than three times the drop of the highest waterfall on land, the Angel Falls in Venezuela.

The mighty Amazon River is longer and carries more water than any other river on land. But the underwater "river", the Antarctic Circumpolar Current that flows around the continent of Antarctica, is the greatest flow of water in the world.

On the Edge

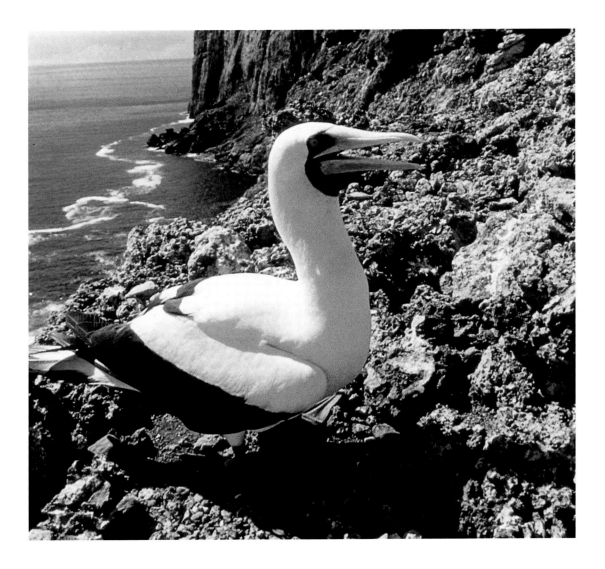

Coastlines are the frontiers between land and sea. They are the most dynamic of all the ocean habitats. Coastlines include sandy beaches and rocky cliffs, as well as the coral reefs and **mangrove** swamps of the tropics. Some animals, such as land crabs, spend their whole lives at the coastline. Others, such as turtles, are just visiting. These creatures may have been washed ashore by accident, or travelled there on purpose to feed or breed. Either way, they will not stay long, and soon return to their real home, the sea.

Life by the Sea

Each spring, when seabirds come ashore to breed, coastlines become like noisy, bustling cities. Funk Island, off the coast of Newfoundland, Canada, attracts gannets, puffins, guillemots, and other seabirds. The birds crowd together in great colonies, jostling for a space on the cliff face where they can lay their eggs. There is safety in numbers; together, the birds are safer, because predators don't want to risk possible attack by hundreds of birds at once.

gannets

Every available space is filled with nests made of sticks and seaweed. Competition for space and food is fierce. When the blue gannet eggs hatch, there are thousands of chicks, naked and black-skinned, needing to be fed. For about three months, the gannet parents journey to and from the sea, bringing back tiny fish for their hungry broods. Then, the parents abandon their young. Hunger drives the parents back to deeper water, where they can dive for fish. The chicks must leave the cliffs to go in search of their own food.

puffins

Mammals of the Sea

walrus

Some sea **mammals** spend their whole lives at sea, but not walruses, seals and sea lions. These mammals live in freezing waters that are far too harsh for their newborn pups, so the animals come ashore to breed. Their pups remain on land until they have enough fat on their bodies to stay warm in the icy seas.

Like the seabirds, sea mammals breed in huge colonies. In Antarctica, up to 10,000 Elephant seals may squeeze onto a single beach each spring. There are reasons for this crowding. Firstly, as the seabirds found, predators are unlikely to attack a large crowd. Also, the animals can find and choose a mate much more easily on the crowded beach than in the open sea.

seal pup

Turtles at Large

Turtles, too, come ashore to breed. They choose sandy beaches where they bury their eggs, and usually return to the beach on which they were born. About half the world's population of Flatbacked turtles gather each year on Crab Island, off the coast of Australia. The turtles bury their soft, leathery eggs in the sand and then hurry back to the sea.

Olive Ridley turtle

baby turtle being
eaten by a gull

When they hatch, the baby turtles will need to struggle down to the safety
of the water, but predators, such as seabirds, are waiting to pounce. Nearly
half of the baby Flatbacks are killed each year.

The Olive Ridley turtle tries to overcome its predators by sheer numbers.
Over a span of just three nights, approximately 100,000 of them
come to the same beach to lay their eggs. Many hatchlings
will still be eaten, but some will survive.

A World of Facts

Did you know?

🐟 Turtles can live to be more than 100 years old.

🐟 Turtles don't have teeth – they have sharp beaks which they use for biting.

🐟 Puffins nest in burrows on grassy cliff-tops. Sometimes, puffins dig their own burrows – but if they find an empty rabbit hole, they may take that over, instead.

🐟 Guillemots live in huge, crowded colonies of over 140,000 birds.

Record breakers

🐟 The world's largest sea turtle is the Leatherback, which can grow to 1.9 metres long and weigh more than 500 kilograms.

Strange but true!

🐟 The sex of a turtle hatchling depends on the temperature of the sand. Where the sand is warm, the turtle will be female. Where the sand is cool, the turtle will be male.

🐟 Walruses and seals spend most of their lives at sea, but they enjoy sunbathing on the beach in summer.

Between the Tides

There is a force powerful enough to move the oceans of the world. It is a force generated by the Moon, 370,000 kilometres away. As the Moon orbits the Earth, its **gravity** sweeps across the face of our planet, creating tides. Tides are the regular rising and falling of the sea. A high tide occurs when the gravity of the moon pulls on the part of the sea that is nearest to it, which causes a low tide somewhere else. On the shore, the portion of the beach between low and high tides is covered and uncovered by the sea twice a day. This makes life difficult for the creatures that live there. At high tide, they can move around in relative safety but at low tide, the hot sun could dry them out, or wading birds could eat them. They need to find ways of protecting themselves.

The Highest Tide

The movement of water in tidal areas creates huge waves and fierce currents. At low tide, shellfish and other tide-pool creatures are swept out to sea, creating rich feeding grounds for herring, whales, dolphins and seabirds. Some creatures, such as clams, sand eels and crabs, bury themselves in the sand during low tide, while others, such as limpets and mussels, close up their shells and cling tightly to the rocks.

The Sally Lightfoot crab, found on the rocky shorelines of Central and South America, has a flattened shell so that it can squeeze into narrow spaces between the rocks and avoid being washed away. When the tide comes in, the crabs come out of hiding and scuttle about, looking for food.

Sally Lightfoot crab

Food for Free

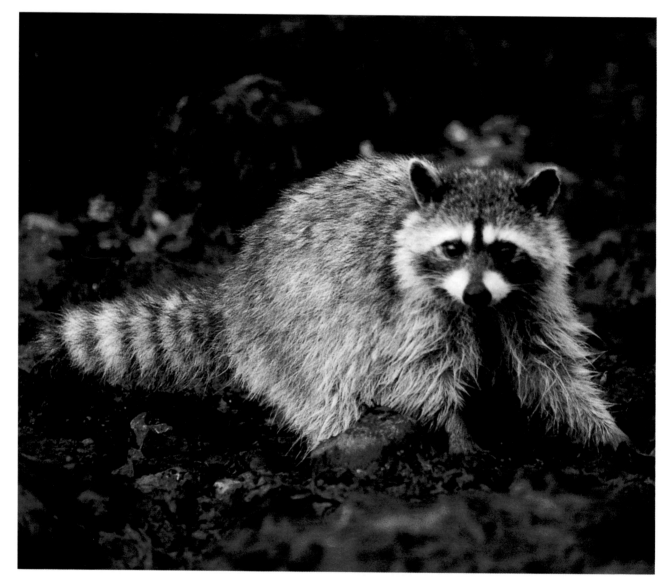

raccoon

The beach can provide a good hunting ground for hungry land animals. When a very low tide uncovers the large, deep-water crabs on Vancouver Island, Canada, raccoons come down to the beach for a feast. The raccoons are able to crack open the crab shells and enjoy a tasty meal. In south east Alaska, grizzly bears dig in the sand for clams.

Colonies of Garden eels live tail-down in burrows in the sand. They push their heads and necks out of the burrows to feed on passing plankton, leaving the rest of their bodies buried beneath the seabed. When they all go out feeding together, they look like a field of waving grass. The slightest disturbance from an approaching predator will send the eels back to their burrows. They will only appear again when they're sure it's safe.

Garden eels

Tropical Waters

Tides vary from place to place. Geographical position determines the level of the tide. In the warm, tropical waters around Florida and the Caribbean, the tides are gentle. One of nature's oddest creatures lives here – a large but harmless mammal called the manatee.

Manatee are sometimes called sea cows, and it is easy to see why – they graze on seagrass and other plants of the shallow waters. Manatees need to eat around 10 per cent of their body weight each day – that's about 80 kilograms of food. They can live in both fresh and salt water, as long as it's warm.

tropical waters, Bahamas

manatee

Sadly, the manatee is an endangered species. In Florida, there are only about 1,900 of these animals left. This is mainly due to the destruction of seagrass beds caused by pollution and coastal development. Manatees are now protected by international law.

A World of Facts

Did you know?

The flow of water in and out of the Bay of Fundy in Canada is the greatest movement of water in the world – the difference between high and low tide can be as much as 16 metres.

A manatee's front teeth are worn down by constant grinding on seagrass. New teeth grow in the back of the manatee's mouth and gradually replace all the old ones.

After the rains on Christmas Island, near Australia, millions of red crabs march from the forests to the sea. They wait on the shore until the tides are right for carrying their eggs to the open ocean. Then they swarm into the sea to **spawn**.

Record breakers

The largest crab on record is a Japanese giant spider crab, which weighed 18 kilograms.

The biggest **jellyfish** in the world, the Lion's Mane jellyfish, is found in the North Atlantic Ocean and the Arctic Ocean. Its body measures 2.4 metres across, and each tentacle is over 36 metres long – that's nearly twice as long as a tennis court!

Strange but true!

Mudskippers are fish that can survive in water and on land. They live in the mudflats of tropical estuaries. When in the water, the mudskipper breathes through its gills. It stores water in its gill chambers and this supplies the oxygen it needs when it's out of the water. Mudskippers can breathe through their skin.

Male fiddler crabs have one huge claw and one smaller claw. They wave the large claw in the air to attract the attention of females, and they feed themselves with the smaller claw. Fiddler crabs live on the beaches of **temperate** and tropical regions of the world.

The Coral Seas

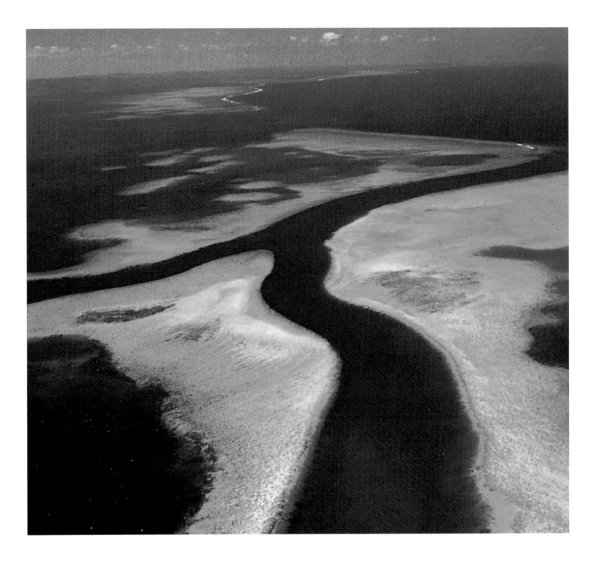

Coral reefs are found in shallow tropical seas. They are made by millions of tiny animals called coral **polyps**, living together in colonies. Each polyp has a soft body with a mouth at the top, ringed by stinging tentacles. Its skeleton is on the outside, and looks like a little limestone cup. **Algae**, aquatic plants including seaweed, provide food for the polyps, which, in turn, provide shelter for the algae. When coral polyps eventually die, live coral grows on top of them, forming a thin layer of colour over the dead coral's white skeleton.

next page: a coral reef

Active Nightlife

Like a big city, the reef is awake and active all night long. As the sea becomes dark, the night shift takes over. This is when many of the predators hunt. Some fish change colour at night, becoming darker so predators can't easily spot them. Moray eels slither around the coral, seeking out their prey by smell. Whitetip sharks use their special electrical sense to detect the slight movements of sleeping fish.

Whitetip sharks

coral

Most corals
feed at night when
there are fewer fish
around to nibble
their tentacles.
When corals catch
passing animal
plankton, they
paralyse their prey using
stinging cells.

Coral polyps can share their
meals – the stomach cavities
of all of the coral polyps are
connected, so they can pass
food along to one another.

Terrorist of the Reef

coral polyps

Even though coral polyps live inside hard skeletons, they are not safe from attack. The most vicious killer of coral is the Crown of Thorns starfish. One of the world's largest starfish, it can grow up to 80 centimetres across.

This dangerous creature has between 6 and 23 arms, all bristling with **toxic** spines and lined with hundreds of suckers. It settles on a coral reef, turns its stomach inside out and eats the polyps in huge quantities. When the starfish moves on, only the coral skeleton is left. In four to six hours, a starfish can eat a patch the size of a dinner plate. A single Crown of Thorns starfish can eat over five square metres of coral in one year. Although the coral polyps cannot run away, they do put up a fight by stinging the starfish. Crabs and shrimps also come to their aid by pinching the predator until it goes away.

Crown of Thorns starfish

A World of Facts

Did you know?

🐟   Corals have existed for approximately 400 million years.

🐟   Coral reefs are found off the shores of over 100 countries. Worldwide, coral reefs are thought to cover around 450,000 square kilometres.

🐟   The biggest threat to coral reefs is not the hungry Crown of Thorns starfish, but people. Overfishing is one problem; people who collect coral to sell as ornaments is another.

Record breakers

🐟   The Australian Great Barrier Reef is the greatest coral structure in the world. It is really a chain of reefs that stretches more than 2,300 kilometres.

🐟   The biggest coral is the Mushroom coral. It is a single polyp that can grow up to 25 centimetres across. It is mobile, able to move along the seabed and turn itself the right way up if a storm knocks it down.

🐟   One of the largest inhabitants of the reef is the giant clam – it can reach 1.4 metres in length.

Strange but true!

🐟   Coral is easily destroyed – even brushing against it can kill it. The anchor of one cruise ship can destroy an area of reef as big as two Olympic swimming pools.

🐟   Scientists consider the Great Barrier Reef to be young – even though it is 10,000 years old!

The Temperate Seas

The temperate seas lie between the polar zones of the Arctic and Antarctic Oceans and the tropical regions near the equator. These waters are home to large seaweeds. The giant of the seaweed world is the kelp that forms underwater forests off the coast of California. Kelp **fronds** can grow to 100 metres in length and provide an ideal home for shoals of fish.

The warm summer sunshine also enables vast "blooms" of plant plankton to grow. Summer is a time of plenty, but, when winter arrives, the water becomes too cold for new plankton to grow or develop. Heavy storms sweep the existing plankton out to sea. Facing such harsh conditions and a lack of available food, many animals swim to warmer waters. They will return when summer comes again.

The Seals of Sable Island

It is January. The seas around Sable Island, Canada, are cold, grey and stormy. The air is full of the sound and smell of grey seals, who are dragging themselves onto the beaches in their thousands. Despite the harsh weather conditions, this is the breeding season for the grey seal.

grey seals

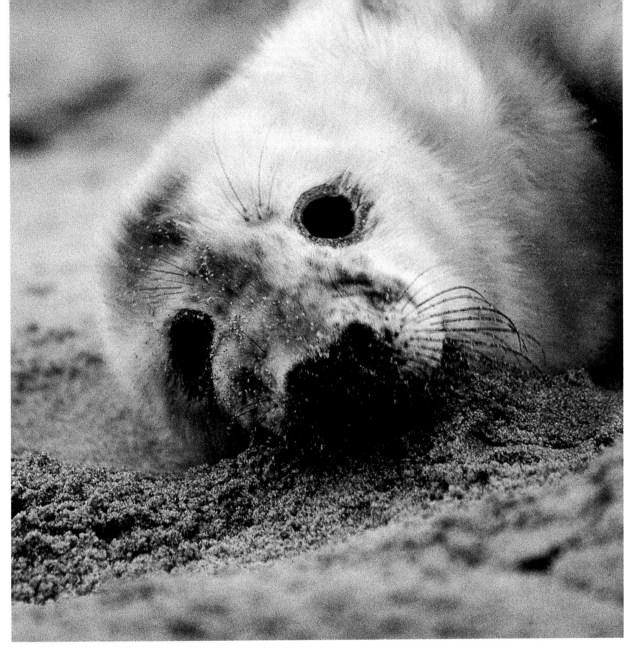

seal pup

For the seals, breeding in winter is not a gamble, but a sensible survival plan. The mother seals have spent the autumn months fattening up on fish, and now they are in top condition. For the first 18 days of their lives, the seal pups will feed on their mother's milk. After that, they must survive on their own blubber until they are ready to go to sea, several weeks later. By the time they are able to hunt for themselves, spring will have arrived, and the food supplies will return.

Herrings and Killer Whales

On the eastern side of the Atlantic, vast shoals of herring have swum into the cold waters of the Norwegian **fjords**, to seek shelter from the stormy winter seas. The local fishermen know the fish are there, and each winter they gather a plentiful harvest.

Out at sea, another group of fishermen is waiting – a **pod** of Killer whales, or Orcas. These streamlined mammals have been stalking the herring for months, eating great quantities of the oily fish.

Killer whales have a wide diet. Apart from herring and other fish, they catch and eat dolphins, seals, and even seabirds and turtles if they can get them. Killer whales can swim huge distances, and are found in every ocean of the world.

Killer whale pod, Norway

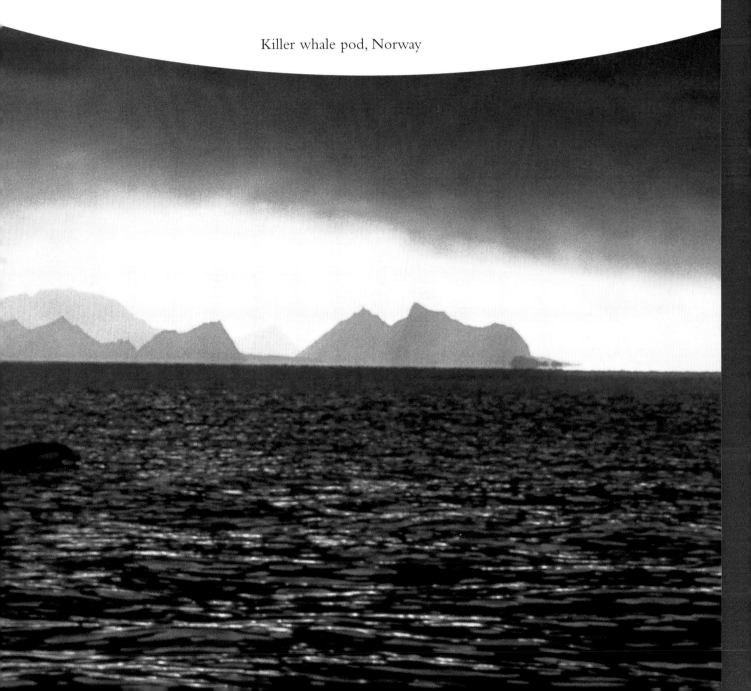

March of the Lobsters

Midsummer has arrived, and the waters of Canada's Atlantic coast are now warmer. But out in the deep, it is still cold – and an army is on the march. This is a column of giant female Atlantic lobsters, each weighing up to 10 kilograms – though some record-breakers have grown to 20 kilograms. The lobsters are heading for the warm, shallow coastal waters to spawn. Each lobster can carry between 10,000 and 30,000 eggs.

Atlantic lobster

In the sea, every creature is a meal for some other living thing, and even the heavily armoured lobster is not safe. The baby lobsters, too, no bigger than plankton, will be sought out by greedy fish. Only very few of the vast numbers of eggs will hatch. Even fewer will survive to grow big enough to move back to the deep oceans.

A World of Facts

Did you know?

 Sea otters living in kelp forests sleep on the surface of the water. They twist a strand of kelp around their bodies to anchor them and ensure they don't get swept out to sea.

 Lobsters can live to be more than 60 years old.

Record breakers

 In March each year, kelp becomes the fastest-growing plant on Earth. It can grow as much as 60 centimetres a day.

 The Killer whale is the biggest member of the dolphin family. It can grow to nearly 10 metres long.

 Atlantic lobsters can grow up to 19 kilograms, but most weigh nearer one kilogram.

Strange but true!

 Killer whales have been known to come up onto the beach to snatch seals.

 Alginates, chemicals produced from kelp, are used in around 70 everyday items including toothpaste and sweets. They are even used to thicken ice cream and paints.

40

Frozen Waters

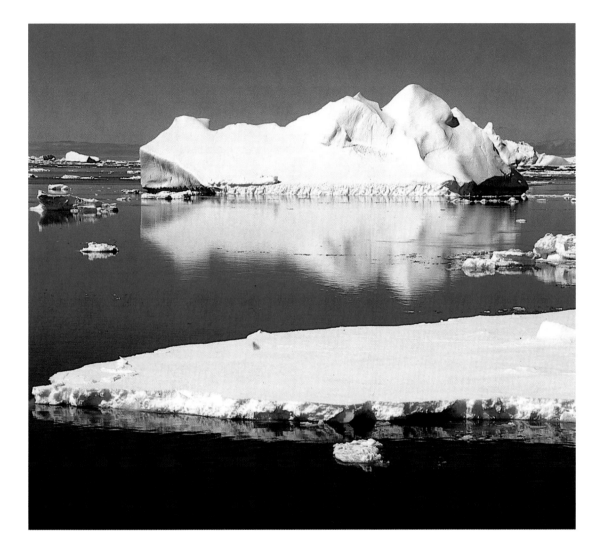

The frozen seas of the Arctic and Antarctic regions seem a cruel and impossible habitat – and yet they are teeming with life. The Arctic and Antarctic are very different from each other. The Antarctic is a frozen continent surrounded by icy seas, while the Arctic is a frozen sea surrounded by land. The animals that live in these two places are different, too, but they share similar survival problems.

Emperor Penguins

It is early winter on the Antarctic Ice Sheet. It is dark, and the temperature is −50°C. A 100-kilometre-per-hour wind is blowing. Without protection, a human being would be dead in minutes. It seems almost impossible for anything to live on these frozen wastes and yet, huddled together for warmth, a colony of Emperor penguins is waiting for their chicks to hatch.

It is the male Emperor penguins that keep the eggs warm; they balance the eggs on their feet and protect them under a pouch of skin. The penguins have developed a special way of keeping out of the worst of the biting wind. The birds are always shuffling around, taking turns to stand on the side of the group that is sheltered from the wind – all the time carrying their one egg balanced on their feet.

As the eggs hatch in the summer, the females return from the sea, each carrying the first meal for its newborn chick in its beak. At last, the hungry males are able to swim out to sea for food. For the next few months, the males and females will take turns feeding and guarding the chicks.

Emperor penguins with chick

Polar Bears

Conditions in the Antarctic might be the toughest in the world, but at least there are no land-based predators. Creatures of the Arctic, such as seals, walruses and small whales, have no such luck. Once they are trapped, a Polar bear's powerful paws can kill them with a single blow.

A sudden freeze has trapped a Beluga whale beneath the Arctic ice. A Polar bear has spotted it. The stranded whale will not last long.

Seals protect their pups as best they can by hiding them in ice caves or breeding on **ice floes** beyond the reach of Polar bears. Even so, only when the ice melts are they reasonably safe from an attack by this dreaded predator. Polar bears can smell meat up to 32 kilometres away and a Polar bear's stomach can hold 20 per cent of its body weight.

right: Polar bear
next page: Humpback whales

A World of Facts

Did you know?

- Polar bears have hair between the pads of their feet to help them get a better grip when running on the ice.

- Although they cannot fly in the air, penguins "fly" underwater at speeds of up to 30 kilometres per hour.

Record breakers

- The Polar bear is the world's largest land meat-eater. A male Polar bear stands up to 2.9 metres tall on its hind legs, and weighs around 400 kilograms.

- A newborn Polar bear cub is about 30 centimetres long, only slightly bigger than a rat.

- Humpback whales can grow to nearly 20 metres long and weigh more than 70 tonnes.

- Emperor penguins are the largest of all penguins, growing to one metre in height and weighing up to 30 kilograms.

Strange but true!

- Most of the time, Polar bears move slowly to avoid overheating, but they can swim at nearly 10 kilometres per hour.

- Beneath its white fur, a Polar bear's skin is actually black.

The Open Ocean

For creatures that make their homes in the open sea, the world must seem a lonely place. The vast, empty ocean stretches from **horizon** to horizon and, apart from scattered islands, the nearest land may be hundreds of kilometres away. Even the seabed may be more than eight kilometres below the surface. There is little plankton out here and, without this, the food chain cannot get started. Such food as there is can be swept away easily by giant storms. Yet, even here, animals survive. "Hot spots" of plankton appear and long-distance travellers such as the Blue shark will cross the whole distance of the Atlantic Ocean to find food.

Cocos Island

Like deserts on land, the open ocean is a habitat where shelter is scarce. Deserts have oases, places with water and plants where travellers can rest. The open oceans have islands that provide a living and resting space for the ocean's travellers. Cocos Island, 160 kilometres from the South American coast, is an extinct volcano. For long-distance travellers, the island is like a motorway service station, where they can fill up with a meal.

Cocos Island

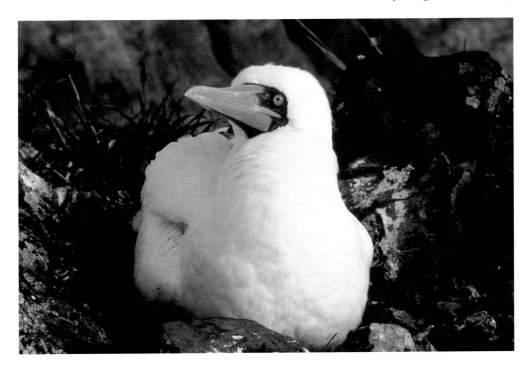

The island provides a roost site for Booby birds, which scour the sea for shoals of baitfish.

Swirling currents concentrate the plankton here. Fish come to feed on the plankton, predators such as sharks come to feed on the fish – and so the food chain builds.

plant plankton floating in the sea

Hitching a Lift

The great oceans are full of hitch-hikers. On the coast of California, mats of floating kelp drift hundreds of kilometres out to sea. Each seaweed raft is a small colony of life. Even a floating log can provide an ocean cruise for a colony of sea barnacles. Barnacles and other **parasites** also cluster on creatures such as whales – and hitch a free ride around the world.

Bowhead whale

Manta ray

Compass
jellyfish

Fish hitch-hike, too. Small fish hide from predators among the
tentacles of stinging jellyfish. Remora, or suckerfish, use their suckers
to stick themselves to Manta rays or Whale sharks, so they don't need
to swim.

The only problem with hitching a ride is being unable to choose where
to go. For plankton, the journey often leads them right into the mouths
of a hungry creature.

Dolphins

Dolphins are the great high jumpers of the open ocean. This behaviour is called **porpoising**, and is a very efficient way of travelling vast distances across the ocean. In the air, the dolphins don't have to push against water resistance, so they are able to breathe freely and continue moving at high speed.

Passengers on ocean liners often see dolphins following or swimming alongside the ship, and sometimes imagine they are simply being friendly. But this isn't the case. The dolphins are saving energy, letting the **bow wave** of the ship pull them along. Dolphins surf, using the pressure created when the front of a moving ship pushes through the water.

Spiner dolphins underwater

A World of Facts

Did you know?

🐟 The word plankton comes from a Greek word, planktos, and means "drifting".

🐟 Australia's Box jelly is the most dangerous jellyfish. Its toxin is stronger than cobra venom and can kill a person in minutes.

🐟 Dolphins can dive down to more than 350 metres and can jump up to six metres out of the water.

Record breakers

🐟 When early sailors crossed the Atlantic and Pacific Oceans, they thought they saw sea monsters. Perhaps they saw the longest fish in the world, the Oarfish, which can grow to a length of six metres or more. The Oarfish has a long, red fin, a horse-like face, and blue gills.

🐟 The world's largest fish, Whale sharks, feed almost exclusively on plankton.

Strange but true!

🐟 Dolphins make a noise about 14 times higher pitched than humans can hear. When the sound waves hit an underwater object, the dolphins can use the echoes produced to locate the object and find out whether it is suitable food.

🐟 Jellyfish are made up of more than 95 per cent water and have no heart, bones or brain, and no real eyes. They have sensors to let them know whether they are heading up or down.

The Deep

Much of the sea is over one kilometre deep. Most of this is completely unexplored – only a few submarines can reach the very deepest parts. By 10 metres down, the **water pressure** has doubled, and the light starts to fade. At 200 metres below the surface, it's almost completely dark and the water is very cold. This is known as the "twilight zone". By 1,000 metres, all light has gone and the pressure is immense. Yet, even here, strange forms of life can thrive.

The Twilight Zone

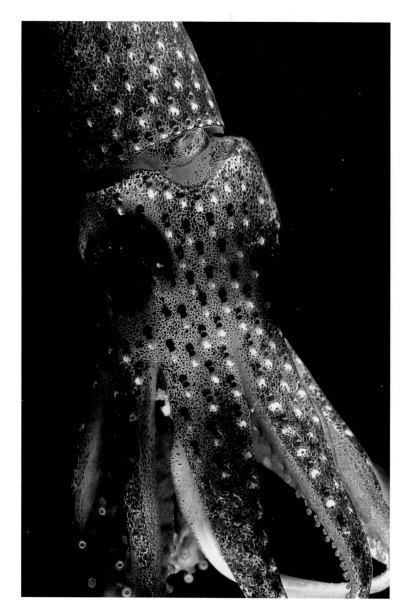

squid

The trick to survival in the twilight zone is to avoid being eaten – by not being seen. Creatures here try to make themselves invisible. Some animals have transparent bodies that are hard to see in the dim light. Even larger creatures such as squid make themselves as see-through as possible. Down here, everyone is a master of disguise.

A Hatchet fish confuses enemies with its mirror-like, flattened sides. But predators will find ways to track down a meal. Many have developed large, extra-sensitive eyes, to make the best use of the faint light.

Hatchet fish

The Dark Zone

Below 1,000 metres, all sunlight has gone. This is an alien world of total darkness. To survive here, in the "dark zone", creatures have had to develop senses other than sight, as well as a few astonishing tricks.

Some of the creatures produce a tiny amount of light themselves. This is called **bioluminescence**. Lantern fish have light-producing areas on their skin and can flash messages to each other in a mysterious Morse-like code of their own. The female Angler fish grows a "fishing rod" at the front of its head. A light dangles at the end of this to attract its next meal. This creature has also solved the problem of finding a mate – the male Angler fish has a super-sensitive "nose" that can sniff out a distant female.

Angler fish

right: hungry Angler fish

A World of Facts

Did you know?

🐟 Until 1930, the greatest ocean depth reached by man was approximately 182 metres.

🐟 In 1934, a record-breaking dive reached 765 metres using a **bathysphere**.

🐟 In 1960, people reached a depth of 10,916 metres. This is still the deepest recorded dive of a submersible craft with people inside.

🐟 Ocean water is always coldest at the bottom where it is usually between 4°C and −1°C.

Record breakers

🐟 The deepest place on Earth is the Mariana Trench at the bottom of the Challenger Deep in the Pacific Ocean. This trench is 11,033 metres deep.

Strange but true!

🐟 Some deep-sea creatures are able to turn red, to protect themselves from predators. The colour red is difficult to see in deep water and makes the animals nearly invisible.

🐟 Angler fish have teeth in their throats to prevent their prey from escaping.

Glossary

Algae Simple, non-flowering plants found in water. Seaweeds are algae.

Bathysphere A chamber which is lowered into the sea by a cable attached to a ship. Scientists can observe ocean plants and animals from inside it.

Bioluminescence Light produced by living things.

Bow wave A wave created by a ship moving quickly through the water.

Current A body of water moving in one direction. Ocean currents are affected by the forces of gravity and wind direction.

Fjord A deep valley carved long ago by a glacier and then filled with sea water.

Food chain The feeding pattern in any particular place, where plants and small creatures feed bigger animals, which in turn feed even bigger animals.

Fronds The leaf or leaf-like part of a palm, fern, or similar plant.

Gravity The force that pulls an object towards the centre of the Earth.

Horizon The line where the land and sky seem to meet.

Ice floes Flat, floating areas of ice.

Jellyfish A marine animal that has a jelly-like, transparent circular body with stinging tentacles around the edge.

Mammal An animal that has hair, and gives birth to and nurses live young.

Mangrove A woody plant which grows between the sea and the land in areas where there are tides.

Parasite A living thing that lives, to its advantage, on or in another living thing.

Plankton Microscopic plants and animals that float in the sea.

Pod A small herd or school of marine animals, especially whales.

Polyp The living part of a coral. When it dies, the polyp leaves behind a chalky shell that gradually builds up to make a coral reef.

Porpoising Travelling through the water by alternately rising above it and submerging.

Predator An animal that kills other creatures for food.

Shoal A large number of fish swimming together.

Spawn Releasing huge quantities of eggs or sperm into the water.

Temperate The part of the world that lies between the tropical and polar zones, where temperatures are moderate or mild. In temperate seas, the surface temperature averages around 20°C.

Toxic Poisonous.

Water pressure The force of water pushing against an object.

First published in 2001 by BBC Worldwide Ltd
Woodlands, 80 Wood Lane, London W12 0TT
Text by David Orme and Helen Bird © 2001 BBC Worldwide Ltd
Design © 2001 BBC Worldwide Ltd
The Blue Planet © BBC 2001

The publishers wish to thank the following for the use of pictures:
The BBC Natural History Unit pp: 1, 12tl, 43, 64 (Doug Allen); 34, 35 (Penny Allen);
26–27, 30–31, 32, 33, 63, 64 (Georgette Douwma); 29, 30tl (Steve Downer); 41 (Hanne and Jens
Eriksen); 8, 44 (Sue Flood); 4–5 (Alistair Fothergill); 12–13 (Jeff Foott); 36–37, 42, 52–53
(Martha Holmes); 10-11,14–15, 16, 46–47, 63 (Ben Osborne); 17, 18–19, 24 (Pete Oxford);
20, 22–23, 63 (Hugh Pearson); 21, 23tr, 25, 53, 56, 57 (Michael Pitts); 28 (Jeff Rotman);
50 (John Ruthven); 49, 51b, 58, 59, 60, 61, 62, 64 (David Shale); 38–39, 40 (Peter Scoones);
45 (Staffan Widstrand)

And also: Florian Graner pp: 9, 51t, 54t, 63; Didier Noirot p:11tr; David Reichert pp: 6, 7, 54–55.